Belongs To

____

BILL TRACKER

MONTH: ___ / ___ CURRENCY: _______

PAID	BILL DETAIL	DUE DATE	AMOUNT			AUTO BILL
			BILL	PAID	UNPAID	
☐						○
☐						○
☐						○
☐						○
☐						○
☐						○
☐						○
☐						○
☐						○
☐						○
☐						○
☐						○
☐						○
☐						○
☐						○
☐						○
☐						○
☐						○
☐						○
☐						○
☐						○
☐						○
☐						○
☐						○
☐						○
		TOTAL				

NOTE:

____

____

BILL TRACKER

MONTH: ___ / ___ CURRENCY: _______

PAID	BILL DETAIL	DUE DATE	AMOUNT			AUTO BILL
			BILL	PAID	UNPAID	
☐						○
☐						○
☐						○
☐						○
☐						○
☐						○
☐						○
☐						○
☐						○
☐						○
☐						○
☐						○
☐						○
☐						○
☐						○
☐						○
☐						○
☐						○
☐						○
☐						○
☐						○
☐						○
☐						○
☐						○
☐						○
		TOTAL				

NOTE:

____

____

BILL TRACKER

MONTH: ___ / ___

CURRENCY: _______

PAID	BILL DETAIL	DUE DATE	AMOUNT			AUTO BILL
			BILL	PAID	UNPAID	
☐						○
☐						○
☐						○
☐						○
☐						○
☐						○
☐						○
☐						○
☐						○
☐						○
☐						○
☐						○
☐						○
☐						○
☐						○
☐						○
☐						○
☐						○
☐						○
☐						○
☐						○
☐						○
☐						○
☐						○
☐						○
		TOTAL				

NOTE:

BILL TRACKER

MONTH: ___ / ___ CURRENCY: _______

PAID	BILL DETAIL	DUE DATE	AMOUNT			AUTO BILL
			BILL	PAID	UNPAID	
☐						○
☐						○
☐						○
☐						○
☐						○
☐						○
☐						○
☐						○
☐						○
☐						○
☐						○
☐						○
☐						○
☐						○
☐						○
☐						○
☐						○
☐						○
☐						○
☐						○
☐						○
☐						○
☐						○
☐						○
☐						○
		TOTAL				

NOTE:

____

____

BILL TRACKER

MONTH: ___ / ___ CURRENCY: _______

PAID	BILL DETAIL	DUE DATE	AMOUNT			AUTO BILL
			BILL	PAID	UNPAID	
☐						○
☐						○
☐						○
☐						○
☐						○
☐						○
☐						○
☐						○
☐						○
☐						○
☐						○
☐						○
☐						○
☐						○
☐						○
☐						○
☐						○
☐						○
☐						○
☐						○
☐						○
☐						○
☐						○
☐						○
☐						○
		TOTAL				

NOTE:

____

____

BILL TRACKER

MONTH: ___ / ___   CURRENCY: _______

PAID	BILL DETAIL	DUE DATE	AMOUNT			AUTO BILL
			BILL	PAID	UNPAID	
☐						○
☐						○
☐						○
☐						○
☐						○
☐						○
☐						○
☐						○
☐						○
☐						○
☐						○
☐						○
☐						○
☐						○
☐						○
☐						○
☐						○
☐						○
☐						○
☐						○
☐						○
☐						○
☐						○
☐						○
☐						○
		TOTAL				

NOTE:

____

____

BILL TRACKER

MONTH: ___ / ___ CURRENCY: _______

PAID	BILL DETAIL	DUE DATE	AMOUNT			AUTO BILL
			BILL	PAID	UNPAID	
☐						○
☐						○
☐						○
☐						○
☐						○
☐						○
☐						○
☐						○
☐						○
☐						○
☐						○
☐						○
☐						○
☐						○
☐						○
☐						○
☐						○
☐						○
☐						○
☐						○
☐						○
☐						○
☐						○
☐						○
☐						○
		TOTAL				

NOTE:

____

____

BILL TRACKER

MONTH: ___ / ___ CURRENCY: _______

PAID	BILL DETAIL	DUE DATE	AMOUNT			AUTO BILL
			BILL	PAID	UNPAID	
☐						○
☐						○
☐						○
☐						○
☐						○
☐						○
☐						○
☐						○
☐						○
☐						○
☐						○
☐						○
☐						○
☐						○
☐						○
☐						○
☐						○
☐						○
☐						○
☐						○
☐						○
☐						○
☐						○
☐						○
☐						○
		TOTAL				

NOTE:

____

____

BILL TRACKER

MONTH: ___ / ___

CURRENCY: _______

PAID	BILL DETAIL	DUE DATE	AMOUNT			AUTO BILL
			BILL	PAID	UNPAID	
☐						○
☐						○
☐						○
☐						○
☐						○
☐						○
☐						○
☐						○
☐						○
☐						○
☐						○
☐						○
☐						○
☐						○
☐						○
☐						○
☐						○
☐						○
☐						○
☐						○
☐						○
☐						○
☐						○
☐						○
☐						○
		TOTAL				

NOTE:

____

____

BILL TRACKER

MONTH: ___ / ___ CURRENCY: _______

PAID	BILL DETAIL	DUE DATE	AMOUNT			AUTO BILL
			BILL	PAID	UNPAID	
☐						○
☐						○
☐						○
☐						○
☐						○
☐						○
☐						○
☐						○
☐						○
☐						○
☐						○
☐						○
☐						○
☐						○
☐						○
☐						○
☐						○
☐						○
☐						○
☐						○
☐						○
☐						○
☐						○
☐						○
☐						○
		TOTAL				

NOTE:

____

____

BILL TRACKER

MONTH: ___ / ___ CURRENCY: _______

PAID	BILL DETAIL	DUE DATE	AMOUNT			AUTO BILL
			BILL	PAID	UNPAID	
☐						○
☐						○
☐						○
☐						○
☐						○
☐						○
☐						○
☐						○
☐						○
☐						○
☐						○
☐						○
☐						○
☐						○
☐						○
☐						○
☐						○
☐						○
☐						○
☐						○
☐						○
☐						○
☐						○
☐						○
☐						○
		TOTAL				

NOTE:

____

____

BILL TRACKER

MONTH: ___ / ___ CURRENCY: _______

PAID	BILL DETAIL	DUE DATE	AMOUNT			AUTO BILL
			BILL	PAID	UNPAID	
☐						○
☐						○
☐						○
☐						○
☐						○
☐						○
☐						○
☐						○
☐						○
☐						○
☐						○
☐						○
☐						○
☐						○
☐						○
☐						○
☐						○
☐						○
☐						○
☐						○
☐						○
☐						○
☐						○
☐						○
☐						○
		TOTAL				

NOTE:

____

____

BILL TRACKER

MONTH: ___ / ___ CURRENCY: _______

PAID	BILL DETAIL	DUE DATE	AMOUNT			AUTO BILL
			BILL	PAID	UNPAID	
☐						○
☐						○
☐						○
☐						○
☐						○
☐						○
☐						○
☐						○
☐						○
☐						○
☐						○
☐						○
☐						○
☐						○
☐						○
☐						○
☐						○
☐						○
☐						○
☐						○
☐						○
☐						○
☐						○
☐						○
☐						○
		TOTAL				

NOTE:

____

____

BILL TRACKER

MONTH: ___ / ___

CURRENCY: _______

PAID	BILL DETAIL	DUE DATE	AMOUNT			AUTO BILL
			BILL	PAID	UNPAID	
☐						○
☐						○
☐						○
☐						○
☐						○
☐						○
☐						○
☐						○
☐						○
☐						○
☐						○
☐						○
☐						○
☐						○
☐						○
☐						○
☐						○
☐						○
☐						○
☐						○
☐						○
☐						○
☐						○
☐						○
☐						○
		TOTAL				

NOTE:

BILL TRACKER

MONTH: ___ / ___

CURRENCY: _______

PAID	BILL DETAIL	DUE DATE	AMOUNT			AUTO BILL
			BILL	PAID	UNPAID	
☐						○
☐						○
☐						○
☐						○
☐						○
☐						○
☐						○
☐						○
☐						○
☐						○
☐						○
☐						○
☐						○
☐						○
☐						○
☐						○
☐						○
☐						○
☐						○
☐						○
☐						○
☐						○
☐						○
☐						○
☐						○
		TOTAL				

NOTE:

BILL TRACKER

MONTH: ___ / ___ CURRENCY: _______

PAID	BILL DETAIL	DUE DATE	AMOUNT			AUTO BILL
			BILL	PAID	UNPAID	
☐						○
☐						○
☐						○
☐						○
☐						○
☐						○
☐						○
☐						○
☐						○
☐						○
☐						○
☐						○
☐						○
☐						○
☐						○
☐						○
☐						○
☐						○
☐						○
☐						○
☐						○
☐						○
☐						○
☐						○
☐						○
		TOTAL				

NOTE:

BILL TRACKER

MONTH: ___ / ___

CURRENCY: _______

PAID	BILL DETAIL	DUE DATE	AMOUNT			AUTO BILL
			BILL	PAID	UNPAID	
☐						○
☐						○
☐						○
☐						○
☐						○
☐						○
☐						○
☐						○
☐						○
☐						○
☐						○
☐						○
☐						○
☐						○
☐						○
☐						○
☐						○
☐						○
☐						○
☐						○
☐						○
☐						○
☐						○
☐						○
☐						○
		TOTAL				

NOTE:

____

____

BILL TRACKER

MONTH: ___ / ___ CURRENCY: _______

PAID	BILL DETAIL	DUE DATE	AMOUNT			AUTO BILL
			BILL	PAID	UNPAID	
☐						○
☐						○
☐						○
☐						○
☐						○
☐						○
☐						○
☐						○
☐						○
☐						○
☐						○
☐						○
☐						○
☐						○
☐						○
☐						○
☐						○
☐						○
☐						○
☐						○
☐						○
☐						○
☐						○
☐						○
☐						○
		TOTAL				

NOTE:

____

____

BILL TRACKER

MONTH: ___ / ___

CURRENCY: _______

PAID	BILL DETAIL	DUE DATE	AMOUNT			AUTO BILL
			BILL	PAID	UNPAID	
☐						○
☐						○
☐						○
☐						○
☐						○
☐						○
☐						○
☐						○
☐						○
☐						○
☐						○
☐						○
☐						○
☐						○
☐						○
☐						○
☐						○
☐						○
☐						○
☐						○
☐						○
☐						○
☐						○
☐						○
☐						○
		TOTAL				

NOTE:

____

____

BILL TRACKER

MONTH: ___ / ___ CURRENCY: _______

PAID	BILL DETAIL	DUE DATE	AMOUNT			AUTO BILL
			BILL	PAID	UNPAID	
☐						◯
☐						◯
☐						◯
☐						◯
☐						◯
☐						◯
☐						◯
☐						◯
☐						◯
☐						◯
☐						◯
☐						◯
☐						◯
☐						◯
☐						◯
☐						◯
☐						◯
☐						◯
☐						◯
☐						◯
☐						◯
☐						◯
☐						◯
☐						◯
☐						◯
		TOTAL				

NOTE:

BILL TRACKER

MONTH: ___ / ___ CURRENCY: _______

PAID	BILL DETAIL	DUE DATE	AMOUNT			AUTO BILL
			BILL	PAID	UNPAID	
☐						○
☐						○
☐						○
☐						○
☐						○
☐						○
☐						○
☐						○
☐						○
☐						○
☐						○
☐						○
☐						○
☐						○
☐						○
☐						○
☐						○
☐						○
☐						○
☐						○
☐						○
☐						○
☐						○
☐						○
☐						○
		TOTAL				

NOTE:

____

____

BILL TRACKER

MONTH: ___ / ___

CURRENCY: _______

PAID	BILL DETAIL	DUE DATE	AMOUNT			AUTO BILL
			BILL	PAID	UNPAID	
☐						○
☐						○
☐						○
☐						○
☐						○
☐						○
☐						○
☐						○
☐						○
☐						○
☐						○
☐						○
☐						○
☐						○
☐						○
☐						○
☐						○
☐						○
☐						○
☐						○
☐						○
☐						○
☐						○
☐						○
☐						○
		TOTAL				

NOTE:

____

____

BILL TRACKER

MONTH: ___ / ___ CURRENCY: _______

PAID	BILL DETAIL	DUE DATE	AMOUNT			AUTO BILL
			BILL	PAID	UNPAID	
☐						○
☐						○
☐						○
☐						○
☐						○
☐						○
☐						○
☐						○
☐						○
☐						○
☐						○
☐						○
☐						○
☐						○
☐						○
☐						○
☐						○
☐						○
☐						○
☐						○
☐						○
☐						○
☐						○
☐						○
☐						○
		TOTAL				

NOTE:

____

____

BILL TRACKER

MONTH: ___ / ___

CURRENCY: _______

PAID	BILL DETAIL	DUE DATE	AMOUNT			AUTO BILL
			BILL	PAID	UNPAID	
☐						◯
☐						◯
☐						◯
☐						◯
☐						◯
☐						◯
☐						◯
☐						◯
☐						◯
☐						◯
☐						◯
☐						◯
☐						◯
☐						◯
☐						◯
☐						◯
☐						◯
☐						◯
☐						◯
☐						◯
☐						◯
☐						◯
☐						◯
☐						◯
☐						◯
		TOTAL				

NOTE:

____

____

BILL TRACKER

MONTH: ___ / ___ CURRENCY: _______

PAID	BILL DETAIL	DUE DATE	AMOUNT			AUTO BILL
			BILL	PAID	UNPAID	
☐						◯
☐						◯
☐						◯
☐						◯
☐						◯
☐						◯
☐						◯
☐						◯
☐						◯
☐						◯
☐						◯
☐						◯
☐						◯
☐						◯
☐						◯
☐						◯
☐						◯
☐						◯
☐						◯
☐						◯
☐						◯
☐						◯
☐						◯
☐						◯
☐						◯
		TOTAL				

NOTE:

____

____

BILL TRACKER

MONTH: ___ / ___ CURRENCY: _______

PAID	BILL DETAIL	DUE DATE	AMOUNT			AUTO BILL
			BILL	PAID	UNPAID	
☐						○
☐						○
☐						○
☐						○
☐						○
☐						○
☐						○
☐						○
☐						○
☐						○
☐						○
☐						○
☐						○
☐						○
☐						○
☐						○
☐						○
☐						○
☐						○
☐						○
☐						○
☐						○
☐						○
☐						○
☐						○
		TOTAL				

NOTE:

____

____

BILL TRACKER

MONTH: ___ / ___ CURRENCY: _______

PAID	BILL DETAIL	DUE DATE	AMOUNT			AUTO BILL
			BILL	PAID	UNPAID	
☐						○
☐						○
☐						○
☐						○
☐						○
☐						○
☐						○
☐						○
☐						○
☐						○
☐						○
☐						○
☐						○
☐						○
☐						○
☐						○
☐						○
☐						○
☐						○
☐						○
☐						○
☐						○
☐						○
☐						○
☐						○
		TOTAL				

NOTE:

____

____

BILL TRACKER

MONTH: ___ / ___ CURRENCY: _______

PAID	BILL DETAIL	DUE DATE	AMOUNT			AUTO BILL
			BILL	PAID	UNPAID	
☐						○
☐						○
☐						○
☐						○
☐						○
☐						○
☐						○
☐						○
☐						○
☐						○
☐						○
☐						○
☐						○
☐						○
☐						○
☐						○
☐						○
☐						○
☐						○
☐						○
☐						○
☐						○
☐						○
☐						○
☐						○
		TOTAL				

NOTE:

____

____

BILL TRACKER

MONTH: ___ / ___   CURRENCY: _______

PAID	BILL DETAIL	DUE DATE	AMOUNT			AUTO BILL
			BILL	PAID	UNPAID	
☐						○
☐						○
☐						○
☐						○
☐						○
☐						○
☐						○
☐						○
☐						○
☐						○
☐						○
☐						○
☐						○
☐						○
☐						○
☐						○
☐						○
☐						○
☐						○
☐						○
☐						○
☐						○
☐						○
☐						○
☐						○
		TOTAL				

NOTE:

____

____

BILL TRACKER

MONTH: ___ / ___

CURRENCY: _______

PAID	BILL DETAIL	DUE DATE	AMOUNT			AUTO BILL
			BILL	PAID	UNPAID	
☐						○
☐						○
☐						○
☐						○
☐						○
☐						○
☐						○
☐						○
☐						○
☐						○
☐						○
☐						○
☐						○
☐						○
☐						○
☐						○
☐						○
☐						○
☐						○
☐						○
☐						○
☐						○
☐						○
☐						○
☐						○
		TOTAL				

NOTE:

____

____

BILL TRACKER

MONTH: ___ / ___ CURRENCY: _______

PAID	BILL DETAIL	DUE DATE	AMOUNT			AUTO BILL
			BILL	PAID	UNPAID	
☐						○
☐						○
☐						○
☐						○
☐						○
☐						○
☐						○
☐						○
☐						○
☐						○
☐						○
☐						○
☐						○
☐						○
☐						○
☐						○
☐						○
☐						○
☐						○
☐						○
☐						○
☐						○
☐						○
☐						○
☐						○
		TOTAL				

NOTE:

____

____

BILL TRACKER

MONTH: ___ / ___ CURRENCY: _______

PAID	BILL DETAIL	DUE DATE	AMOUNT			AUTO BILL
			BILL	PAID	UNPAID	
☐						○
☐						○
☐						○
☐						○
☐						○
☐						○
☐						○
☐						○
☐						○
☐						○
☐						○
☐						○
☐						○
☐						○
☐						○
☐						○
☐						○
☐						○
☐						○
☐						○
☐						○
☐						○
☐						○
☐						○
☐						○
		TOTAL				

NOTE:

____

____

BILL TRACKER

MONTH: ___ / ___ CURRENCY: _______

PAID	BILL DETAIL	DUE DATE	AMOUNT			AUTO BILL
			BILL	PAID	UNPAID	
☐						○
☐						○
☐						○
☐						○
☐						○
☐						○
☐						○
☐						○
☐						○
☐						○
☐						○
☐						○
☐						○
☐						○
☐						○
☐						○
☐						○
☐						○
☐						○
☐						○
☐						○
☐						○
☐						○
☐						○
☐						○
		TOTAL				

NOTE:

BILL TRACKER

MONTH: ___ / ___ CURRENCY: _______

PAID	BILL DETAIL	DUE DATE	AMOUNT			AUTO BILL
			BILL	PAID	UNPAID	
☐						◯
☐						◯
☐						◯
☐						◯
☐						◯
☐						◯
☐						◯
☐						◯
☐						◯
☐						◯
☐						◯
☐						◯
☐						◯
☐						◯
☐						◯
☐						◯
☐						◯
☐						◯
☐						◯
☐						◯
☐						◯
☐						◯
☐						◯
☐						◯
☐						◯
		TOTAL				

NOTE:

____

____

BILL TRACKER

MONTH: ___ / ___ CURRENCY: _______

PAID	BILL DETAIL	DUE DATE	AMOUNT			AUTO BILL
			BILL	PAID	UNPAID	
☐						○
☐						○
☐						○
☐						○
☐						○
☐						○
☐						○
☐						○
☐						○
☐						○
☐						○
☐						○
☐						○
☐						○
☐						○
☐						○
☐						○
☐						○
☐						○
☐						○
☐						○
☐						○
☐						○
☐						○
☐						○
		TOTAL				

NOTE:

____

____

BILL TRACKER

MONTH: ___ / ___ CURRENCY: _______

PAID	BILL DETAIL	DUE DATE	AMOUNT			AUTO BILL
			BILL	PAID	UNPAID	
☐						○
☐						○
☐						○
☐						○
☐						○
☐						○
☐						○
☐						○
☐						○
☐						○
☐						○
☐						○
☐						○
☐						○
☐						○
☐						○
☐						○
☐						○
☐						○
☐						○
☐						○
☐						○
☐						○
☐						○
☐						○
		TOTAL				

NOTE:

____

____

BILL TRACKER

MONTH: ___ / ___ CURRENCY: _______

PAID	BILL DETAIL	DUE DATE	AMOUNT			AUTO BILL
			BILL	PAID	UNPAID	
☐						○
☐						○
☐						○
☐						○
☐						○
☐						○
☐						○
☐						○
☐						○
☐						○
☐						○
☐						○
☐						○
☐						○
☐						○
☐						○
☐						○
☐						○
☐						○
☐						○
☐						○
☐						○
☐						○
☐						○
☐						○
		TOTAL				

NOTE:

____

____

BILL TRACKER

MONTH: ___ / ___ CURRENCY: _______

PAID	BILL DETAIL	DUE DATE	AMOUNT			AUTO BILL
			BILL	PAID	UNPAID	
☐						○
☐						○
☐						○
☐						○
☐						○
☐						○
☐						○
☐						○
☐						○
☐						○
☐						○
☐						○
☐						○
☐						○
☐						○
☐						○
☐						○
☐						○
☐						○
☐						○
☐						○
☐						○
☐						○
☐						○
☐						○
		TOTAL				

NOTE:

____

____

BILL TRACKER

MONTH: ___ / ___

CURRENCY: _______

PAID	BILL DETAIL	DUE DATE	AMOUNT			AUTO BILL
			BILL	PAID	UNPAID	
☐						○
☐						○
☐						○
☐						○
☐						○
☐						○
☐						○
☐						○
☐						○
☐						○
☐						○
☐						○
☐						○
☐						○
☐						○
☐						○
☐						○
☐						○
☐						○
☐						○
☐						○
☐						○
☐						○
☐						○
☐						○
		TOTAL				

NOTE:

____

____

BILL TRACKER

MONTH: ___ / ___ CURRENCY: _______

PAID	BILL DETAIL	DUE DATE	AMOUNT			AUTO BILL
			BILL	PAID	UNPAID	
☐						○
☐						○
☐						○
☐						○
☐						○
☐						○
☐						○
☐						○
☐						○
☐						○
☐						○
☐						○
☐						○
☐						○
☐						○
☐						○
☐						○
☐						○
☐						○
☐						○
☐						○
☐						○
☐						○
☐						○
☐						○
		TOTAL				

NOTE:

BILL TRACKER

MONTH: ___ / ___ CURRENCY: _______

PAID	BILL DETAIL	DUE DATE	AMOUNT			AUTO BILL
			BILL	PAID	UNPAID	
☐						○
☐						○
☐						○
☐						○
☐						○
☐						○
☐						○
☐						○
☐						○
☐						○
☐						○
☐						○
☐						○
☐						○
☐						○
☐						○
☐						○
☐						○
☐						○
☐						○
☐						○
☐						○
☐						○
☐						○
☐						○
		TOTAL				

NOTE:

BILL TRACKER

MONTH: ___ / ___ CURRENCY: _______

PAID	BILL DETAIL	DUE DATE	AMOUNT			AUTO BILL
			BILL	PAID	UNPAID	
☐						○
☐						○
☐						○
☐						○
☐						○
☐						○
☐						○
☐						○
☐						○
☐						○
☐						○
☐						○
☐						○
☐						○
☐						○
☐						○
☐						○
☐						○
☐						○
☐						○
☐						○
☐						○
☐						○
☐						○
☐						○
		TOTAL				

NOTE:

BILL TRACKER

MONTH: ___ / ___ CURRENCY: _______

PAID	BILL DETAIL	DUE DATE	AMOUNT			AUTO BILL
			BILL	PAID	UNPAID	
☐						○
☐						○
☐						○
☐						○
☐						○
☐						○
☐						○
☐						○
☐						○
☐						○
☐						○
☐						○
☐						○
☐						○
☐						○
☐						○
☐						○
☐						○
☐						○
☐						○
☐						○
☐						○
☐						○
☐						○
☐						○
		TOTAL				

NOTE:

____

____

BILL TRACKER

MONTH: ___ / ___ CURRENCY: _______

PAID	BILL DETAIL	DUE DATE	AMOUNT			AUTO BILL
			BILL	PAID	UNPAID	
☐						○
☐						○
☐						○
☐						○
☐						○
☐						○
☐						○
☐						○
☐						○
☐						○
☐						○
☐						○
☐						○
☐						○
☐						○
☐						○
☐						○
☐						○
☐						○
☐						○
☐						○
☐						○
☐						○
☐						○
☐						○
		TOTAL				

NOTE:

___

___

BILL TRACKER

MONTH: ___ / ___ CURRENCY: _______

PAID	BILL DETAIL	DUE DATE	AMOUNT			AUTO BILL
			BILL	PAID	UNPAID	
☐						○
☐						○
☐						○
☐						○
☐						○
☐						○
☐						○
☐						○
☐						○
☐						○
☐						○
☐						○
☐						○
☐						○
☐						○
☐						○
☐						○
☐						○
☐						○
☐						○
☐						○
☐						○
☐						○
☐						○
☐						○
		TOTAL				

NOTE:

____

____

BILL TRACKER

MONTH: ___ / ___

CURRENCY: _______

PAID	BILL DETAIL	DUE DATE	AMOUNT			AUTO BILL
			BILL	PAID	UNPAID	
☐						○
☐						○
☐						○
☐						○
☐						○
☐						○
☐						○
☐						○
☐						○
☐						○
☐						○
☐						○
☐						○
☐						○
☐						○
☐						○
☐						○
☐						○
☐						○
☐						○
☐						○
☐						○
☐						○
☐						○
☐						○
		TOTAL				

NOTE:

BILL TRACKER

MONTH: ___ / ___

CURRENCY: _______

PAID	BILL DETAIL	DUE DATE	AMOUNT			AUTO BILL
			BILL	PAID	UNPAID	
☐						○
☐						○
☐						○
☐						○
☐						○
☐						○
☐						○
☐						○
☐						○
☐						○
☐						○
☐						○
☐						○
☐						○
☐						○
☐						○
☐						○
☐						○
☐						○
☐						○
☐						○
☐						○
☐						○
☐						○
☐						○
		TOTAL				

NOTE:

____

____

BILL TRACKER

MONTH: ___ / ___ CURRENCY: _______

PAID	BILL DETAIL	DUE DATE	AMOUNT			AUTO BILL
			BILL	PAID	UNPAID	
☐						○
☐						○
☐						○
☐						○
☐						○
☐						○
☐						○
☐						○
☐						○
☐						○
☐						○
☐						○
☐						○
☐						○
☐						○
☐						○
☐						○
☐						○
☐						○
☐						○
☐						○
☐						○
☐						○
☐						○
☐						○
		TOTAL				

NOTE:

BILL TRACKER

MONTH: ___ / ___ CURRENCY: _______

PAID	BILL DETAIL	DUE DATE	AMOUNT			AUTO BILL
			BILL	PAID	UNPAID	
☐						○
☐						○
☐						○
☐						○
☐						○
☐						○
☐						○
☐						○
☐						○
☐						○
☐						○
☐						○
☐						○
☐						○
☐						○
☐						○
☐						○
☐						○
☐						○
☐						○
☐						○
☐						○
☐						○
☐						○
☐						○
		TOTAL				

NOTE:

____

____

BILL TRACKER

MONTH: ___ / ___ CURRENCY: _______

PAID	BILL DETAIL	DUE DATE	AMOUNT			AUTO BILL
			BILL	PAID	UNPAID	
☐						○
☐						○
☐						○
☐						○
☐						○
☐						○
☐						○
☐						○
☐						○
☐						○
☐						○
☐						○
☐						○
☐						○
☐						○
☐						○
☐						○
☐						○
☐						○
☐						○
☐						○
☐						○
☐						○
☐						○
☐						○
		TOTAL				

NOTE:

BILL TRACKER

MONTH: ___ / ___ CURRENCY: _______

PAID	BILL DETAIL	DUE DATE	AMOUNT			AUTO BILL
			BILL	PAID	UNPAID	
☐						○
☐						○
☐						○
☐						○
☐						○
☐						○
☐						○
☐						○
☐						○
☐						○
☐						○
☐						○
☐						○
☐						○
☐						○
☐						○
☐						○
☐						○
☐						○
☐						○
☐						○
☐						○
☐						○
☐						○
☐						○
		TOTAL				

NOTE:

____

____

BILL TRACKER

MONTH: ___ / ___

CURRENCY: _______

PAID	BILL DETAIL	DUE DATE	AMOUNT			AUTO BILL
			BILL	PAID	UNPAID	
☐						○
☐						○
☐						○
☐						○
☐						○
☐						○
☐						○
☐						○
☐						○
☐						○
☐						○
☐						○
☐						○
☐						○
☐						○
☐						○
☐						○
☐						○
☐						○
☐						○
☐						○
☐						○
☐						○
☐						○
☐						○
		TOTAL				

NOTE:

____

____

BILL TRACKER

MONTH: ___ / ___

CURRENCY: _______

PAID	BILL DETAIL	DUE DATE	AMOUNT			AUTO BILL
			BILL	PAID	UNPAID	
☐						○
☐						○
☐						○
☐						○
☐						○
☐						○
☐						○
☐						○
☐						○
☐						○
☐						○
☐						○
☐						○
☐						○
☐						○
☐						○
☐						○
☐						○
☐						○
☐						○
☐						○
☐						○
☐						○
☐						○
☐						○
		TOTAL				

NOTE:

____

____

BILL TRACKER

MONTH: ___ / ___ CURRENCY: _______

PAID	BILL DETAIL	DUE DATE	AMOUNT			AUTO BILL
			BILL	PAID	UNPAID	
☐						○
☐						○
☐						○
☐						○
☐						○
☐						○
☐						○
☐						○
☐						○
☐						○
☐						○
☐						○
☐						○
☐						○
☐						○
☐						○
☐						○
☐						○
☐						○
☐						○
☐						○
☐						○
☐						○
☐						○
☐						○
		TOTAL				

NOTE:

____

____

BILL TRACKER

MONTH: ___ / ___ CURRENCY: _______

PAID	BILL DETAIL	DUE DATE	AMOUNT			AUTO BILL
			BILL	PAID	UNPAID	
		TOTAL				

NOTE:

BILL TRACKER

MONTH: ___ / ___

CURRENCY: _______

PAID	BILL DETAIL	DUE DATE	AMOUNT			AUTO BILL
			BILL	PAID	UNPAID	
☐						○
☐						○
☐						○
☐						○
☐						○
☐						○
☐						○
☐						○
☐						○
☐						○
☐						○
☐						○
☐						○
☐						○
☐						○
☐						○
☐						○
☐						○
☐						○
☐						○
☐						○
☐						○
☐						○
☐						○
☐						○
		TOTAL				

NOTE:

____

____

BILL TRACKER

MONTH: ___ / ___ CURRENCY: _______

PAID	BILL DETAIL	DUE DATE	AMOUNT			AUTO BILL
			BILL	PAID	UNPAID	
☐						○
☐						○
☐						○
☐						○
☐						○
☐						○
☐						○
☐						○
☐						○
☐						○
☐						○
☐						○
☐						○
☐						○
☐						○
☐						○
☐						○
☐						○
☐						○
☐						○
☐						○
☐						○
☐						○
☐						○
☐						○
		TOTAL				

NOTE:

____

____

BILL TRACKER

MONTH: ___ / ___ CURRENCY: _______

PAID	BILL DETAIL	DUE DATE	AMOUNT			AUTO BILL
			BILL	PAID	UNPAID	
☐						◯
☐						◯
☐						◯
☐						◯
☐						◯
☐						◯
☐						◯
☐						◯
☐						◯
☐						◯
☐						◯
☐						◯
☐						◯
☐						◯
☐						◯
☐						◯
☐						◯
☐						◯
☐						◯
☐						◯
☐						◯
☐						◯
☐						◯
☐						◯
☐						◯
		TOTAL				

NOTE:

BILL TRACKER

MONTH: ___ / ___

CURRENCY: _______

PAID	BILL DETAIL	DUE DATE	AMOUNT			AUTO BILL
			BILL	PAID	UNPAID	
☐						○
☐						○
☐						○
☐						○
☐						○
☐						○
☐						○
☐						○
☐						○
☐						○
☐						○
☐						○
☐						○
☐						○
☐						○
☐						○
☐						○
☐						○
☐						○
☐						○
☐						○
☐						○
☐						○
☐						○
☐						○
		TOTAL				

NOTE:

____

____

BILL TRACKER

MONTH: ___ / ___ CURRENCY: _______

PAID	BILL DETAIL	DUE DATE	AMOUNT			AUTO BILL
			BILL	PAID	UNPAID	
☐						○
☐						○
☐						○
☐						○
☐						○
☐						○
☐						○
☐						○
☐						○
☐						○
☐						○
☐						○
☐						○
☐						○
☐						○
☐						○
☐						○
☐						○
☐						○
☐						○
☐						○
☐						○
☐						○
☐						○
☐						○
		TOTAL				

NOTE:

____

____

BILL TRACKER

MONTH: ___ / ___ CURRENCY: _______

PAID	BILL DETAIL	DUE DATE	AMOUNT			AUTO BILL
			BILL	PAID	UNPAID	
☐						○
☐						○
☐						○
☐						○
☐						○
☐						○
☐						○
☐						○
☐						○
☐						○
☐						○
☐						○
☐						○
☐						○
☐						○
☐						○
☐						○
☐						○
☐						○
☐						○
☐						○
☐						○
☐						○
☐						○
☐						○
		TOTAL				

NOTE:

____

____

BILL TRACKER

MONTH: ___ / ___ CURRENCY: _______

PAID	BILL DETAIL	DUE DATE	AMOUNT			AUTO BILL
			BILL	PAID	UNPAID	
☐						○
☐						○
☐						○
☐						○
☐						○
☐						○
☐						○
☐						○
☐						○
☐						○
☐						○
☐						○
☐						○
☐						○
☐						○
☐						○
☐						○
☐						○
☐						○
☐						○
☐						○
☐						○
☐						○
☐						○
☐						○
		TOTAL				

NOTE:

____

____

BILL TRACKER

MONTH: ___ / ___ CURRENCY: _______

PAID	BILL DETAIL	DUE DATE	AMOUNT			AUTO BILL
			BILL	PAID	UNPAID	
☐						○
☐						○
☐						○
☐						○
☐						○
☐						○
☐						○
☐						○
☐						○
☐						○
☐						○
☐						○
☐						○
☐						○
☐						○
☐						○
☐						○
☐						○
☐						○
☐						○
☐						○
☐						○
☐						○
☐						○
☐						○
		TOTAL				

NOTE:

BILL TRACKER

MONTH: ___ / ___

CURRENCY: _______

PAID	BILL DETAIL	DUE DATE	AMOUNT			AUTO BILL
			BILL	PAID	UNPAID	
		TOTAL				

NOTE:

BILL TRACKER

MONTH: ___ / ___

CURRENCY: _______

PAID	BILL DETAIL	DUE DATE	AMOUNT			AUTO BILL
			BILL	PAID	UNPAID	
☐						○
☐						○
☐						○
☐						○
☐						○
☐						○
☐						○
☐						○
☐						○
☐						○
☐						○
☐						○
☐						○
☐						○
☐						○
☐						○
☐						○
☐						○
☐						○
☐						○
☐						○
☐						○
☐						○
☐						○
☐						○
		TOTAL				

NOTE:

____

____

BILL TRACKER

MONTH: ___ / ___

CURRENCY: _______

PAID	BILL DETAIL	DUE DATE	AMOUNT			AUTO BILL
			BILL	PAID	UNPAID	
☐						○
☐						○
☐						○
☐						○
☐						○
☐						○
☐						○
☐						○
☐						○
☐						○
☐						○
☐						○
☐						○
☐						○
☐						○
☐						○
☐						○
☐						○
☐						○
☐						○
☐						○
☐						○
☐						○
☐						○
☐						○
		TOTAL				

NOTE:

BILL TRACKER

MONTH: ___ / ___ CURRENCY: _______

PAID	BILL DETAIL	DUE DATE	AMOUNT			AUTO BILL
			BILL	PAID	UNPAID	
☐						○
☐						○
☐						○
☐						○
☐						○
☐						○
☐						○
☐						○
☐						○
☐						○
☐						○
☐						○
☐						○
☐						○
☐						○
☐						○
☐						○
☐						○
☐						○
☐						○
☐						○
☐						○
☐						○
☐						○
☐						○
		TOTAL				

NOTE:

____

____

BILL TRACKER

MONTH: ___ / ___ CURRENCY: _______

PAID	BILL DETAIL	DUE DATE	AMOUNT			AUTO BILL
			BILL	PAID	UNPAID	
☐						○
☐						○
☐						○
☐						○
☐						○
☐						○
☐						○
☐						○
☐						○
☐						○
☐						○
☐						○
☐						○
☐						○
☐						○
☐						○
☐						○
☐						○
☐						○
☐						○
☐						○
☐						○
☐						○
☐						○
☐						○
		TOTAL				

NOTE:

___

___

BILL TRACKER

MONTH: ___ / ___ CURRENCY: _______

PAID	BILL DETAIL	DUE DATE	AMOUNT			AUTO BILL
			BILL	PAID	UNPAID	
☐						○
☐						○
☐						○
☐						○
☐						○
☐						○
☐						○
☐						○
☐						○
☐						○
☐						○
☐						○
☐						○
☐						○
☐						○
☐						○
☐						○
☐						○
☐						○
☐						○
☐						○
☐						○
☐						○
☐						○
☐						○
		TOTAL				

NOTE:

____

____

BILL TRACKER

MONTH: ___ / ___ CURRENCY: _______

PAID	BILL DETAIL	DUE DATE	AMOUNT			AUTO BILL
			BILL	PAID	UNPAID	
☐						○
☐						○
☐						○
☐						○
☐						○
☐						○
☐						○
☐						○
☐						○
☐						○
☐						○
☐						○
☐						○
☐						○
☐						○
☐						○
☐						○
☐						○
☐						○
☐						○
☐						○
☐						○
☐						○
☐						○
☐						○
		TOTAL				

NOTE:

____

____

BILL TRACKER

MONTH: ___ / ___ CURRENCY: _______

PAID	BILL DETAIL	DUE DATE	AMOUNT			AUTO BILL
			BILL	PAID	UNPAID	
☐						○
☐						○
☐						○
☐						○
☐						○
☐						○
☐						○
☐						○
☐						○
☐						○
☐						○
☐						○
☐						○
☐						○
☐						○
☐						○
☐						○
☐						○
☐						○
☐						○
☐						○
☐						○
☐						○
☐						○
☐						○
		TOTAL				

NOTE:

____

____

BILL TRACKER

MONTH: ___ / ___ CURRENCY: _______

PAID	BILL DETAIL	DUE DATE	AMOUNT			AUTO BILL
			BILL	PAID	UNPAID	
☐						○
☐						○
☐						○
☐						○
☐						○
☐						○
☐						○
☐						○
☐						○
☐						○
☐						○
☐						○
☐						○
☐						○
☐						○
☐						○
☐						○
☐						○
☐						○
☐						○
☐						○
☐						○
☐						○
☐						○
☐						○
		TOTAL				

NOTE:

BILL TRACKER

MONTH: ___ / ___ CURRENCY: _______

PAID	BILL DETAIL	DUE DATE	AMOUNT			AUTO BILL
			BILL	PAID	UNPAID	
☐						○
☐						○
☐						○
☐						○
☐						○
☐						○
☐						○
☐						○
☐						○
☐						○
☐						○
☐						○
☐						○
☐						○
☐						○
☐						○
☐						○
☐						○
☐						○
☐						○
☐						○
☐						○
☐						○
☐						○
☐						○
		TOTAL				

NOTE:

BILL TRACKER

MONTH: ___ / ___ CURRENCY: _______

PAID	BILL DETAIL	DUE DATE	AMOUNT			AUTO BILL
			BILL	PAID	UNPAID	
☐						○
☐						○
☐						○
☐						○
☐						○
☐						○
☐						○
☐						○
☐						○
☐						○
☐						○
☐						○
☐						○
☐						○
☐						○
☐						○
☐						○
☐						○
☐						○
☐						○
☐						○
☐						○
☐						○
☐						○
☐						○
		TOTAL				

NOTE:

BILL TRACKER

MONTH: ___ / ___ CURRENCY: _______

PAID	BILL DETAIL	DUE DATE	AMOUNT			AUTO BILL
			BILL	PAID	UNPAID	
☐						○
☐						○
☐						○
☐						○
☐						○
☐						○
☐						○
☐						○
☐						○
☐						○
☐						○
☐						○
☐						○
☐						○
☐						○
☐						○
☐						○
☐						○
☐						○
☐						○
☐						○
☐						○
☐						○
☐						○
☐						○
		TOTAL				

NOTE:

____

____

BILL TRACKER

MONTH: ___ / ___

CURRENCY: _______

PAID	BILL DETAIL	DUE DATE	AMOUNT			AUTO BILL
			BILL	PAID	UNPAID	
☐						○
☐						○
☐						○
☐						○
☐						○
☐						○
☐						○
☐						○
☐						○
☐						○
☐						○
☐						○
☐						○
☐						○
☐						○
☐						○
☐						○
☐						○
☐						○
☐						○
☐						○
☐						○
☐						○
☐						○
☐						○
		TOTAL				

NOTE:

BILL TRACKER

MONTH: ___ / ___

CURRENCY: _______

PAID	BILL DETAIL	DUE DATE	AMOUNT			AUTO BILL
			BILL	PAID	UNPAID	
☐						○
☐						○
☐						○
☐						○
☐						○
☐						○
☐						○
☐						○
☐						○
☐						○
☐						○
☐						○
☐						○
☐						○
☐						○
☐						○
☐						○
☐						○
☐						○
☐						○
☐						○
☐						○
☐						○
☐						○
☐						○
		TOTAL				

NOTE:

____

____

BILL TRACKER

MONTH: ___ / ___ CURRENCY: _______

PAID	BILL DETAIL	DUE DATE	AMOUNT			AUTO BILL
			BILL	PAID	UNPAID	
☐						○
☐						○
☐						○
☐						○
☐						○
☐						○
☐						○
☐						○
☐						○
☐						○
☐						○
☐						○
☐						○
☐						○
☐						○
☐						○
☐						○
☐						○
☐						○
☐						○
☐						○
☐						○
☐						○
☐						○
☐						○
		TOTAL				

NOTE:

____

____

BILL TRACKER

MONTH: ___ / ___

CURRENCY: _______

PAID	BILL DETAIL	DUE DATE	AMOUNT			AUTO BILL
			BILL	PAID	UNPAID	
☐						○
☐						○
☐						○
☐						○
☐						○
☐						○
☐						○
☐						○
☐						○
☐						○
☐						○
☐						○
☐						○
☐						○
☐						○
☐						○
☐						○
☐						○
☐						○
☐						○
☐						○
☐						○
☐						○
☐						○
☐						○
		TOTAL				

NOTE:

____

____

BILL TRACKER

MONTH: ___ / ___ CURRENCY: _______

PAID	BILL DETAIL	DUE DATE	AMOUNT			AUTO BILL
			BILL	PAID	UNPAID	
☐						○
☐						○
☐						○
☐						○
☐						○
☐						○
☐						○
☐						○
☐						○
☐						○
☐						○
☐						○
☐						○
☐						○
☐						○
☐						○
☐						○
☐						○
☐						○
☐						○
☐						○
☐						○
☐						○
☐						○
☐						○
		TOTAL				

NOTE:

____

____

BILL TRACKER

MONTH: ___ / ___ CURRENCY: _______

PAID	BILL DETAIL	DUE DATE	AMOUNT			AUTO BILL
			BILL	PAID	UNPAID	
☐						○
☐						○
☐						○
☐						○
☐						○
☐						○
☐						○
☐						○
☐						○
☐						○
☐						○
☐						○
☐						○
☐						○
☐						○
☐						○
☐						○
☐						○
☐						○
☐						○
☐						○
☐						○
☐						○
☐						○
☐						○
		TOTAL				

NOTE:

____

____

BILL TRACKER

MONTH: ___ / ___ CURRENCY: _______

PAID	BILL DETAIL	DUE DATE	AMOUNT			AUTO BILL
			BILL	PAID	UNPAID	
☐						○
☐						○
☐						○
☐						○
☐						○
☐						○
☐						○
☐						○
☐						○
☐						○
☐						○
☐						○
☐						○
☐						○
☐						○
☐						○
☐						○
☐						○
☐						○
☐						○
☐						○
☐						○
☐						○
☐						○
☐						○
		TOTAL				

NOTE:

____

____

BILL TRACKER

MONTH: ___ / ___

CURRENCY: _______

PAID	BILL DETAIL	DUE DATE	AMOUNT			AUTO BILL
			BILL	PAID	UNPAID	
☐						○
☐						○
☐						○
☐						○
☐						○
☐						○
☐						○
☐						○
☐						○
☐						○
☐						○
☐						○
☐						○
☐						○
☐						○
☐						○
☐						○
☐						○
☐						○
☐						○
☐						○
☐						○
☐						○
☐						○
☐						○
		TOTAL				

NOTE:

____

____

BILL TRACKER

MONTH: ___ / ___ CURRENCY: _______

PAID	BILL DETAIL	DUE DATE	AMOUNT			AUTO BILL
			BILL	PAID	UNPAID	
☐						○
☐						○
☐						○
☐						○
☐						○
☐						○
☐						○
☐						○
☐						○
☐						○
☐						○
☐						○
☐						○
☐						○
☐						○
☐						○
☐						○
☐						○
☐						○
☐						○
☐						○
☐						○
☐						○
☐						○
☐						○
		TOTAL				

NOTE:

____

____

BILL TRACKER

MONTH: ___ / ___ CURRENCY: _______

PAID	BILL DETAIL	DUE DATE	AMOUNT			AUTO BILL
			BILL	PAID	UNPAID	
☐						○
☐						○
☐						○
☐						○
☐						○
☐						○
☐						○
☐						○
☐						○
☐						○
☐						○
☐						○
☐						○
☐						○
☐						○
☐						○
☐						○
☐						○
☐						○
☐						○
☐						○
☐						○
☐						○
☐						○
☐						○
		TOTAL				

NOTE:

____

____

BILL TRACKER

MONTH: ___ / ___ CURRENCY: _______

PAID	BILL DETAIL	DUE DATE	AMOUNT			AUTO BILL
			BILL	PAID	UNPAID	
☐						○
☐						○
☐						○
☐						○
☐						○
☐						○
☐						○
☐						○
☐						○
☐						○
☐						○
☐						○
☐						○
☐						○
☐						○
☐						○
☐						○
☐						○
☐						○
☐						○
☐						○
☐						○
☐						○
☐						○
☐						○
		TOTAL				

NOTE:

____

____

BILL TRACKER

MONTH: ___ / ___

CURRENCY: _______

PAID	BILL DETAIL	DUE DATE	AMOUNT			AUTO BILL
			BILL	PAID	UNPAID	
☐						○
☐						○
☐						○
☐						○
☐						○
☐						○
☐						○
☐						○
☐						○
☐						○
☐						○
☐						○
☐						○
☐						○
☐						○
☐						○
☐						○
☐						○
☐						○
☐						○
☐						○
☐						○
☐						○
☐						○
☐						○
		TOTAL				

NOTE:

____

____

BILL TRACKER

MONTH: ___ / ___ CURRENCY: _______

PAID	BILL DETAIL	DUE DATE	AMOUNT			AUTO BILL
			BILL	PAID	UNPAID	
☐						○
☐						○
☐						○
☐						○
☐						○
☐						○
☐						○
☐						○
☐						○
☐						○
☐						○
☐						○
☐						○
☐						○
☐						○
☐						○
☐						○
☐						○
☐						○
☐						○
☐						○
☐						○
☐						○
☐						○
☐						○
		TOTAL				

NOTE:

___

___

BILL TRACKER

MONTH: ___ / ___ CURRENCY: _______

PAID	BILL DETAIL	DUE DATE	AMOUNT			AUTO BILL
			BILL	PAID	UNPAID	
☐						○
☐						○
☐						○
☐						○
☐						○
☐						○
☐						○
☐						○
☐						○
☐						○
☐						○
☐						○
☐						○
☐						○
☐						○
☐						○
☐						○
☐						○
☐						○
☐						○
☐						○
☐						○
☐						○
☐						○
☐						○
		TOTAL				

NOTE:

____

____

BILL TRACKER

MONTH: ___ / ___ CURRENCY: _______

PAID	BILL DETAIL	DUE DATE	AMOUNT			AUTO BILL
			BILL	PAID	UNPAID	
☐						○
☐						○
☐						○
☐						○
☐						○
☐						○
☐						○
☐						○
☐						○
☐						○
☐						○
☐						○
☐						○
☐						○
☐						○
☐						○
☐						○
☐						○
☐						○
☐						○
☐						○
☐						○
☐						○
☐						○
☐						○
		TOTAL				

NOTE:

____

____

BILL TRACKER

MONTH: ___ / ___

CURRENCY: _______

PAID	BILL DETAIL	DUE DATE	AMOUNT			AUTO BILL
			BILL	PAID	UNPAID	
☐						○
☐						○
☐						○
☐						○
☐						○
☐						○
☐						○
☐						○
☐						○
☐						○
☐						○
☐						○
☐						○
☐						○
☐						○
☐						○
☐						○
☐						○
☐						○
☐						○
☐						○
☐						○
☐						○
☐						○
☐						○
		TOTAL				

NOTE:

____

____

BILL TRACKER

MONTH: ___ / ___   CURRENCY: _______

PAID	BILL DETAIL	DUE DATE	AMOUNT			AUTO BILL
			BILL	PAID	UNPAID	
☐						○
☐						○
☐						○
☐						○
☐						○
☐						○
☐						○
☐						○
☐						○
☐						○
☐						○
☐						○
☐						○
☐						○
☐						○
☐						○
☐						○
☐						○
☐						○
☐						○
☐						○
☐						○
☐						○
☐						○
☐						○
		TOTAL				

NOTE:

BILL TRACKER

MONTH: ___ / ___ CURRENCY: _______

PAID	BILL DETAIL	DUE DATE	AMOUNT			AUTO BILL
			BILL	PAID	UNPAID	
☐						○
☐						○
☐						○
☐						○
☐						○
☐						○
☐						○
☐						○
☐						○
☐						○
☐						○
☐						○
☐						○
☐						○
☐						○
☐						○
☐						○
☐						○
☐						○
☐						○
☐						○
☐						○
☐						○
☐						○
☐						○
		TOTAL				

NOTE:

____

____

BILL TRACKER

MONTH: ___ / ___

CURRENCY: _______

PAID	BILL DETAIL	DUE DATE	AMOUNT			AUTO BILL
			BILL	PAID	UNPAID	
☐						○
☐						○
☐						○
☐						○
☐						○
☐						○
☐						○
☐						○
☐						○
☐						○
☐						○
☐						○
☐						○
☐						○
☐						○
☐						○
☐						○
☐						○
☐						○
☐						○
☐						○
☐						○
☐						○
☐						○
☐						○
		TOTAL				

NOTE:

BILL TRACKER

MONTH: ___ / ___ CURRENCY: _______

PAID	BILL DETAIL	DUE DATE	AMOUNT			AUTO BILL
			BILL	PAID	UNPAID	
☐						○
☐						○
☐						○
☐						○
☐						○
☐						○
☐						○
☐						○
☐						○
☐						○
☐						○
☐						○
☐						○
☐						○
☐						○
☐						○
☐						○
☐						○
☐						○
☐						○
☐						○
☐						○
☐						○
☐						○
☐						○
		TOTAL				

NOTE:

____

____

BILL TRACKER

MONTH: ___ / ___

CURRENCY: _______

PAID	BILL DETAIL	DUE DATE	AMOUNT			AUTO BILL
			BILL	PAID	UNPAID	
☐						○
☐						○
☐						○
☐						○
☐						○
☐						○
☐						○
☐						○
☐						○
☐						○
☐						○
☐						○
☐						○
☐						○
☐						○
☐						○
☐						○
☐						○
☐						○
☐						○
☐						○
☐						○
☐						○
☐						○
☐						○
		TOTAL				

NOTE:

____

____

BILL TRACKER

MONTH: ___ / ___

CURRENCY: _______

PAID	BILL DETAIL	DUE DATE	AMOUNT			AUTO BILL
			BILL	PAID	UNPAID	
☐						○
☐						○
☐						○
☐						○
☐						○
☐						○
☐						○
☐						○
☐						○
☐						○
☐						○
☐						○
☐						○
☐						○
☐						○
☐						○
☐						○
☐						○
☐						○
☐						○
☐						○
☐						○
☐						○
☐						○
☐						○
		TOTAL				

NOTE:

____

____

BILL TRACKER

MONTH: ___ / ___ CURRENCY: _______

PAID	BILL DETAIL	DUE DATE	AMOUNT			AUTO BILL
			BILL	PAID	UNPAID	
☐						○
☐						○
☐						○
☐						○
☐						○
☐						○
☐						○
☐						○
☐						○
☐						○
☐						○
☐						○
☐						○
☐						○
☐						○
☐						○
☐						○
☐						○
☐						○
☐						○
☐						○
☐						○
☐						○
☐						○
☐						○
		TOTAL				

NOTE:

BILL TRACKER

MONTH: ___ / ___ CURRENCY: _______

PAID	BILL DETAIL	DUE DATE	AMOUNT			AUTO BILL
			BILL	PAID	UNPAID	
☐						○
☐						○
☐						○
☐						○
☐						○
☐						○
☐						○
☐						○
☐						○
☐						○
☐						○
☐						○
☐						○
☐						○
☐						○
☐						○
☐						○
☐						○
☐						○
☐						○
☐						○
☐						○
☐						○
☐						○
☐						○
		TOTAL				

NOTE:

____

____

BILL TRACKER

MONTH: ___ / ___

CURRENCY: _______

PAID	BILL DETAIL	DUE DATE	AMOUNT			AUTO BILL
			BILL	PAID	UNPAID	
		TOTAL				

NOTE:

____

____

BILL TRACKER

MONTH: ___ / ___

CURRENCY: _______

PAID	BILL DETAIL	DUE DATE	AMOUNT			AUTO BILL
			BILL	PAID	UNPAID	
☐						○
☐						○
☐						○
☐						○
☐						○
☐						○
☐						○
☐						○
☐						○
☐						○
☐						○
☐						○
☐						○
☐						○
☐						○
☐						○
☐						○
☐						○
☐						○
☐						○
☐						○
☐						○
☐						○
☐						○
☐						○
		TOTAL				

NOTE:

____

____

BILL TRACKER

MONTH: ___ / ___ CURRENCY: _______

PAID	BILL DETAIL	DUE DATE	AMOUNT			AUTO BILL
			BILL	PAID	UNPAID	
☐						○
☐						○
☐						○
☐						○
☐						○
☐						○
☐						○
☐						○
☐						○
☐						○
☐						○
☐						○
☐						○
☐						○
☐						○
☐						○
☐						○
☐						○
☐						○
☐						○
☐						○
☐						○
☐						○
☐						○
☐						○
		TOTAL				

NOTE:

____

____

BILL TRACKER

MONTH: ___ / ___

CURRENCY: _______

PAID	BILL DETAIL	DUE DATE	AMOUNT			AUTO BILL
			BILL	PAID	UNPAID	
☐						○
☐						○
☐						○
☐						○
☐						○
☐						○
☐						○
☐						○
☐						○
☐						○
☐						○
☐						○
☐						○
☐						○
☐						○
☐						○
☐						○
☐						○
☐						○
☐						○
☐						○
☐						○
☐						○
☐						○
☐						○
		TOTAL				

NOTE:

____

____

BILL TRACKER

MONTH: ___ / ___ CURRENCY: _______

PAID	BILL DETAIL	DUE DATE	AMOUNT			AUTO BILL
			BILL	PAID	UNPAID	
☐						○
☐						○
☐						○
☐						○
☐						○
☐						○
☐						○
☐						○
☐						○
☐						○
☐						○
☐						○
☐						○
☐						○
☐						○
☐						○
☐						○
☐						○
☐						○
☐						○
☐						○
☐						○
☐						○
☐						○
☐						○
		TOTAL				

NOTE:

____

____

BILL TRACKER

MONTH: ___ / ___ CURRENCY: _______

PAID	BILL DETAIL	DUE DATE	AMOUNT			AUTO BILL
			BILL	PAID	UNPAID	
		TOTAL				

NOTE:

____

____

BILL TRACKER

MONTH: ___ / ___ CURRENCY: _______

PAID	BILL DETAIL	DUE DATE	AMOUNT			AUTO BILL
			BILL	PAID	UNPAID	
☐						○
☐						○
☐						○
☐						○
☐						○
☐						○
☐						○
☐						○
☐						○
☐						○
☐						○
☐						○
☐						○
☐						○
☐						○
☐						○
☐						○
☐						○
☐						○
☐						○
☐						○
☐						○
☐						○
☐						○
☐						○
		TOTAL				

NOTE:

BILL TRACKER

MONTH: ___ / ___

CURRENCY: _______

PAID	BILL DETAIL	DUE DATE	AMOUNT			AUTO BILL
			BILL	PAID	UNPAID	
☐						○
☐						○
☐						○
☐						○
☐						○
☐						○
☐						○
☐						○
☐						○
☐						○
☐						○
☐						○
☐						○
☐						○
☐						○
☐						○
☐						○
☐						○
☐						○
☐						○
☐						○
☐						○
☐						○
☐						○
☐						○
		TOTAL				

NOTE:

____

____

BILL TRACKER

MONTH: ___ / ___ CURRENCY: _______

PAID	BILL DETAIL	DUE DATE	AMOUNT			AUTO BILL
			BILL	PAID	UNPAID	
☐						○
☐						○
☐						○
☐						○
☐						○
☐						○
☐						○
☐						○
☐						○
☐						○
☐						○
☐						○
☐						○
☐						○
☐						○
☐						○
☐						○
☐						○
☐						○
☐						○
☐						○
☐						○
☐						○
☐						○
☐						○
		TOTAL				

NOTE:

____

____

CPSIA information can be obtained
at www.ICGtesting.com
Printed in the USA
LVHW060945261221
707158LV00013B/942